S.S./640.]

SALVAGE.

(Revised Edition.)

(ISSUED BY QUARTERMASTER GENERAL'S BRANCH.)

FRANCE,
October, 1918.

www.firesteppublishing.com

FireStep Publishing
Gemini House
136-140 Old Shoreham Road
Brighton
BN3 7BD

www.firesteppublishing.com

First published by the General Staff, War Office 1918.
First published in this format by FireStep Editions,
an imprint of FireStep Publishing, in association with
the National Army Museum, 2013.

www.nam.ac.uk

ISBN 978-1-908487-65-0

Cover design FireStep Publishing
Typeset by FireStep Publishing
Printed and bound in Great Britain

Please note: *In producing in facsimile from original historical documents, any imperfections may be reproduced and the quality may be lower than modern typesetting or cartographic standards.*

S.S./640.]

SALVAGE.

(Revised Edition.)

(ISSUED BY QUARTERMASTER GENERAL'S BRANCH.)

FRANCE,
October, 1918.

FOREWORD.

1. *The Need for Economy.*—It must always be borne in mind that this is essentially a war of national endurance and that everything done to conserve our resources is helping towards victory and peace. Economy in material is only second in importance to economy in man-power.

2. *Why the Need has become Greater.*—One must not be misled by the fact that material has hitherto always seemed abundant; it is becoming more and more difficult to supply everything that is required. We began this war with a small army supported by a large industrial population, a great mercantile marine, immense national wealth and the produce of the world. We have now a huge army supported by a depleted industrial population, a mercantile marine that works under considerable difficulties, and resources of money and material that have already been severely drained. Waste at this stage is therefore criminal and dangerous, and the most thorough and loyal co-operation in the cause of economy on the part of all ranks has become a matter of vital importance.

3. *The German Side of the Question.*—It must be remembered that the enemy is keenly alive to the need for economy; he has indeed to overcome difficulties even greater than we have. He is doing his utmost to husband and increase his own resources, and at the same time is using every means in his power, by submarine and aerial attack, to destroy ours. Every neglect of economy is therefore a blow struck for Germany.

4. *Principles of Economy.*—The first economy is to refrain from demanding material not absolutely required. The second economy is to treat all material used with the greatest care. The third economy is to return all unwanted material, all material requiring repair, all unserviceable material, and all "empties." The fourth economy is to salve all material that has become derelict. To observe these principles is an obligation which rests on every officer, N.C.O., and man in the army. It may be remarked that the more strictly the first three economies mentioned above are carried out, the less will remain to be done under the fourth heading. The salvage of derelict material is in fact a last resort, the necessity for which should be reduced to a minimum.

5. *The Value of Salvage.*—No salvage work is without result. The developments since the first edition of this pamphlet was put into print show that there is practically nothing of the débris of the battlefield that is not of value as salvage. Returned surplus stores are reissued from the Base, and the demands on the United Kingdom and for shipping are thereby reduced. Large workshops exist at the Bases and at Home, where all kinds of stores can be repaired; stores that are beyond repair have usually valuable parts, and as a last resort almost every substance has a value as "scrap." Valuable by-products, too, are extracted from many apparently useless substances. And all empty boxes, fired cartridge cases, and the like, can be filled again at Home.

6. *Special Instructions.*—General Routine Orders are published from time to time drawing attention to items of which the salvage is particularly urgent at the moment, and giving the latest instructions with regard to the sorting and consignment of special categories of salved material. Attention is particularly directed to G.R.O. 4513 ("Ammunition 'Empties' and Components, packing and return of"), to G.R.O. 4704 ("Scrap Metal, Salvage and Evacuation of"), and to "Extracts from General Routine Orders, Part II.," Chapter V., "Salvage and Economies."

SALVAGE.

I.—Organization.

1. The system adopted in the British Armies in France for the recovery of the "By-Products of War," is based on the co-operation of two agents:—

(1) The troops whose duty it is, following administrative orders, to collect and return to railhead *through the normal channels of supply* all unserviceable or surplus stores.

(2) An organization to supplement the work of the troops by the collection of derelict material.

2. The utilization or disposal of recovered material is arranged by the various Departments of Supply in accordance with instructions issued by the Quartermaster General at General Headquarters.

3. The object of Salvage is that nothing that can be used shall go to waste. To this end it is necessary to arrange, in the first place, the collection of all abandoned material, except "dud" shells or bombs, and in the second, its disposal by those channels through which it will be brought into use again with the least delay and to the best advantage.

4. Experience has shown that this problem is best solved by dividing it into two phases:—

(i.) *Routine Salvage*—*i.e.*, collection and disposal of all material which has become derelict by reason of:—

(*a*) Normal wastage, which is continuous in all areas occupied by troops.

(*b*) Active operations.

(ii.) *Special Area Salvage*—*i.e.*, the dismantlement of dug-outs, mine-galleries, hutments, etc., and the collection of any remaining derelict material in places which have passed out of the zone of active operations.

5. The former depends for its success on the close co-operation of the troops; its work lies chiefly in Forward Areas and goes on day by day without reference to the main features of the military situation as part of the daily routine of modern warfare.

6. The initiation of the latter, on the other hand, including as it does the dismantlement of defensive works and hutted camps, is dependent on the military situation, and can only come into full operation in those regions where a forward movement has rendered fortified positions unnecessary. Thus the localities in which these operations can take place are variable in extent, and, as a corollary, the amount of labour for their performance is not a constant factor.

7. Consideration of these points of divergence shows that whereas the one demands an organization in close touch with the fighting units, and a permanent connection with the areas in which it works, the other is best served by an organization which can be expanded or shrunk at will as its field of operations changes.

8. For these reasons, a separate and distinct organization has been provided for each phase:—

(i.) For "Routine Salvage" it consists of:—

(*a*) A Corps Troops Area Salvage Unit permanently allotted to each Corps.

(*b*) A Divisional Salvage Unit with each Division.

PRESS A—12/18—8500S—17,500.

(ii.) For "Special Area Salvage," a permanent supervising and directing staff, under an officer called "The Special Area Salvage Officer," has been formed. To this nucleus, transport and unskilled labour is attached as required and available.

9. Direction and control of "Routine Salvage" operations are vested in the Quartermaster General's Branch of the Staff.

10. To supervise "Special Area Salvage" operations and to co-ordinate methods and arrangements for collection, use and disposal of Salvage generally, a department under an officer known as the "Controller of Salvage" has been formed.

11. As far as "Special Area Salvage" is concerned, this department is executive, but, as regards "Routine Salvage" operations and disposal of salved material, it is a consultative and advisory body to the Quartermaster General at General Headquarters.

12. To ensure that the two organizations for Salvage will not overlap the Controller of Salvage, acting under instructions from the Quartermaster General at General Headquarters, will define the localities and dates for Salvage operations to be placed under the Special Area Salvage Officer.

13. Diagrams showing the organization for Salvage in the British Armies in France form Appendices I. and II.

II.—Routine Salvage.

1. "Routine Salvage" operations comprise:—

(i.) Collection of derelict material in Army and other areas occupied by troops.

(ii.) Sorting and, in conjunction with the departments concerned, disposal of collected material.

2. Their success depends on:—

(i.) The care with which the initial details and arrangements have been planned.

(ii.) The completeness of the instructions which have been issued.

(iii.) The energy with which those instructions are put into practice.

This is especially the case during offensive operations, when the bulk of material to be handled and the difficulties of collection are both greatly increased.

3. The ground covered by "Routine Salvage" operations is divisible into two zones:—

(i.) The zone of operations, *i.e.*—Forward Areas.

(ii.) The zone occupied by troops in camps and billets, *i.e.*—Back Areas and areas on the Lines of Communication.

Collection of Salvage in the Zone of Operations.

4. The collection of Salvage in the zone of operations will be carried out by the officers in charge of Divisional Salvage Units.

5. The co-operation of units in collection, and in provision of transport, is of primary importance, and Divisional Salvage Officers will keep in close touch with all Officers Commanding Units in their respective Areas. Their aim should be to give all possible assistance to Commanding Officers, and, in return, to secure their interest and help.

6. Administrative orders as to the return of unserviceable or surplus stores are framed to meet the various situations as they arise. By their full observance, not merely to the letter but in the spirit, units can lessen the difficulties of supply, and so render immense assistance to the Empire.

7. Unserviceable articles sent back through the normal channels of supply reach the repair shops or depots more rapidly and in better condition than those abandoned and collected by Salvage Units at some later date; consequently they can be brought into further use more rapidly and at less cost in labour and money.

8. Commanding Officers are responsible that every endeavour is made to prevent loss of Government property. Sandbags hung up at intervals in the trench system have been found useful for the reception of small articles.

9. The Royal Artillery should send all empty ammunition boxes and packages, fired brass cartridge cases and other used ammunition components, from the gun positions to Ammunition Railheads.

When new positions are taken up every endeavour must be made to bring up all unfired ammunition to the new position. The Battery Commander is responsible for carrying this out whenever possible. If it is not possible for him to do so, he will report the location of the position and the quantity of ammunition left behind, in order that arrangements may be made by the Division or Corps for its subsequent removal.

10. In the French Army, for the evacuation of fired 75 mm. cartridge cases from batteries to refilling point, a certain number of sacks, made of strong cloth, are issued and carried on the battery wagons. Each holds 25 empty cases. The sacks are made up in bundles of 50, and each battery carries two bundles. It is calculated that one bundle is sufficient to contain the empty cartridge cases of one day's firing (1,200 rounds). Artillery parks of the Corps d'Armées are provided with enough sacks to replace those used or lost by the batteries.

11. It is also primarily the duty of the troops to see that no abandoned article is left derelict, and the principle that no fit man or prisoner of war should return from the Front Area without bringing some salved article with him should be enforced. At the same time everything should be done to help the soldier to salve by making the work as easy as possible for him, and Divisional Salvage Officers should make arrangements for the reception of Salvage collected by the troops.

Salvage Receiving Stations.

12. For this purpose, in consultation with Officers Commanding Units, "Salvage Receiving Stations" should be established by the sides of light railways, roads, duck-boards, or other avenues of communication. As the fullest use should be made of transport returning empty from the Front, these Stations are best placed on a return traffic route.

13. A tired man is far more likely to bring in, say, an abandoned rifle if he knows that he has not to carry it far before he can leave it to be cleared by the personnel of the Salvage Organization. For this reason a certain number of "Salvage Receiving Stations" should be established as far forward as possible, especially during offensive operations.

14. They should be conspicuously marked by a notice board with "Salvage Receiving Station" painted on it. In muddy or boggy country it has been found well to provide them with receptacles for Salvage. An efficient type can be made out of wire netting, but in this case boxes or sandbags should also be provided for small articles.

During Offensive Operations.

15. Normally, the collection of Salvage is best effected by a subdivision of the field of operations into areas, and by a systematic clearance of the ground, area by area. In this case all derelict material in an area is collected without distinction as to its relative value or importance, and the work is continued in that area until the officer in charge of Salvage operations is satisfied that it is thoroughly clean. But during offensive operations the primary object of Salvage is to collect perishable stores and those particular articles which are in constant demand at such a time to replace the wastage of battle, either immediately or after repair.

16. An efficient system enables units to be equipped or supplied in the shortest possible time with many things which they urgently need, and thus materially assists in prosecution of the battle.

17. Some of the most important of these articles, such as rifles and ammunition of all kinds, deteriorate with exposure; consequently rapidity of collection is an essential.

18. When it can be arranged, oil baths should be erected, and rifles, bayonets, etc., passed through the bath and roughly cleaned as soon as possible. Rifles should invariably be inspected as they are received to make sure they are not loaded.

19. As soon as the situation permits, collection of material on the battlefield should begin. Salvage Officers should always reconnoitre the ground beforehand in order that:—

(i.) Those places where Salvage is in large quantity and easily collected may be worked first.

(ii.) The requisite amount of labour be allotted to each locality.

(iii.) The best arrangements be made for evacuation of Salvage.

(iv.) Priority be given to perishable stores and those categories of Salvage of most importance at the moment.

20. Salvage Officers should keep in touch with the course of operations to know where the most severe fighting has been, and, consequently, where the bulk of the Salvage is likely to be. This will quicken the work of reconnaissance and allow collecting parties to begin work with the least delay.

21. The types of Salvage which are most important during offensive operations will generally be found in the zone of the infantry attack. Here the Salvage is never localized to the same extent as it is in evacuated gun positions, and, consequently, far more ground has to be covered in the course of collection, whilst the surface of the ground has frequently been so destroyed that salvage has to be carried by hand for a considerable distance before transport can be obtained. For collection and evacuation of Salvage to the nearest traffic route under these conditions the Yukon Pack has been found useful; by its adoption labour is saved and the material collected is correspondingly increased.

22. Salvage of rifles, equipment, etc., on the field of battle should be carried out in conjunction with burial parties. Rifles should be inspected and, if necessary, unloaded at the same time.

After an Advance.

23. For the collection of Salvage on the battlefield after an advance, the Divisional Salvage Officer should divide his area into suitable sub-areas, and concentrate his labour upon them in rotation. When one sub-area has been thoroughly cleaned he should move his men to the next, and so on. Sub-areas

should be arranged so that they are bounded on at least one side by a light railway or road, if possible a return traffic circuit.

24. To clean a sub-area it will generally be best to work in small groups of 6 to 10 men, each under a non-commissioned officer. Every man should carry two haversacks for loose S.A.A. rounds, S.A.A. cases, and other small articles.

25. If necessary, one or more of these groups should be specifically allotted to the task of collecting fired cartridges cases and other artillery ammunition components, as these are localized in the old gun positions. Cartridge cases should be packed in sandbags, 8 in each bag. The filled bags should then be taken to the side of the road or Decauville track. Each man should fill and carry 100 to 150 sandbags per day, according to the amount of ground covered and its condition.

All shell holes, etc., near evacuated gun positions should be examined, as fired cases and sandbags filled with small components have frequently been found in them.

26. The remainder of the groups should be detailed for collection of general salvage; for this purpose the sub-area should be divided into strips and a group should be detailed to sweep each strip up to the boundary road or Decauville, by the side of which the collected salvage should be placed. Flags may be used to mark the boundaries of each strip.

27. Non-commissioned officers in charge of collecting groups will report daily to the Divisional Salvage Officer:—

(i.) Number and nature of articles collected.

(ii.) Number and nature of articles despatched to main Salvage Dumps.

(iii.) In cases of apparently preventable waste, the places where they have been found.

28. The Divisional Salvage Officer should mark off on a large scale map all portions of his area which, by personnel inspection, he knows to be clear.

29. Men employed on collection of Salvage should take their mid-day meal with them and eat it on the ground, but should have a hot meal in the evening after their return.

In Back Areas and in Areas on the Lines of Communication.

30. In Back Areas, and on the Lines of Communication, it is the duty of Commandants and Town Majors to inspect all billets and camps in their areas, to arrange for collection of material left behind, and to notify Headquarters concerned as to the size and position of such dumps, so that arrangements may be made for their removal or disposal.

31. Certificates that camps and billets are clean should be rendered by Commanding Officers on arrival and departure.

32. Particular notice should be taken of preventable waste, and every case reported without delay to the Headquarters of the Corps or Army concerned, or of the Lines of Communication, to fix responsibility, and for disciplinary action to be taken. To stop preventable waste is the duty of every officer and N.C.O.

33. All inhabitants should be warned to hand to the Civil Authorities any British Stores which may come into their possession.

Evacuation of Salvage from Receiving Stations.

34. Salvage must never be allowed to accumulate at "Salvage Receiving Stations" or by the sides of roads and light railways. The Staff should arrange, as far as possible, for provision of sufficient transport to evacuate it daily to Main Salvage Dumps; full use should be made of all road and rail transport returning from the Front empty.

35. Officers of the organization for Salvage are responsible that transport is not delayed longer than necessary; accordingly they must see that there are enough men to load the Salvage, and to off-load at the main Salvage Dumps.

36. In some cases, it may be possible to save road transport by arranging an intermediate trans-shipping station at a point on a light railway system, between "Receiving Stations" and "Main Salvage Dumps."

37. This method will decrease road miles but increase light railway miles and handling; therefore its adoption would depend largely on the relative difficulty of obtaining the two types of transport and on the labour available.

38. When trans-shipping stations are used, they should be sited to serve a group of "Receiving Stations."

Main Salvage Dumps.

39. Every Main Salvage Dump should be at some suitable point on a light or broad gauge railway, such as an advanced railhead, a main reailhead, or a broad gauge trans-shipping station.

40. The number of Main Salvage Dumps in an area allotted to a Corps should not exceed the minimum which will provide the requisite facilities for :—

(i.) Evacuating Salvage from the "Salvage Receiving Stations," and from the sides of roads or light railways where it has been placed by collecting parties.

(ii.) Sorting and despatching it to its destination by rail or road.

Sorting and Disposal of Salvage.

41. Salved material will be sorted and disposed of at Main Salvage Dumps. Engineer Stores, Ordnance Stores and Supplies will be separate from one another, and a particular part of the dump will be allotted to each of these main categories.

42. Salvage must be dealt with promptly as it is all-important for it to be brought into use again with the least possibly delay.

43. During offensive operations, priority of despatch should be given to articles which can be immediately used in battle. At such times, it will probably be necessary to augment the personnel at the dumps to handle the increased bulk of material.

All Salvage Officers must be in closest touch with the various departments which control the supply of material to the troops. They should inform them daily as to the nature and quantities of serviceable and repairable articles in their dumps, and obtain instructions as to their disposal.

44. Oil baths should be constructed and rifles, bayonets, etc., should be thoroughly examined and cleaned as soon as received. Great care should be taken in handling rifles as the barrels are easily bent.

45. At least one man with a thorough knowledge and training in the examination of bombs and grenades should be stationed at every Main Salvage Dump to examine bombs, and to remove detonators when necessary.

46. In consultation with officers of the departments concerned, salved material will be sorted into three categories:—

(i.) Fit for immediate reissue.

(ii.) Fit for reissue after repair.

(iii.) Fit for produce.

47. These will be dealt with under directions of the departmental officer concerned. On no account will any article be issued direct to units from Salvage Dumps, except on the written authority of an officer authorized to make such issues.

48. The bulk of the material collected by "Routine Salvage" operations consists of Ordnance Stores, and officers of that department should visit Main Salvage Dumps daily.

49. Salvage Officers will take receipts for all articles issued to units or handed over to departmental officers, and will send waybills with all articles despatched by rail or road.

50. It will be found a great advantage if each man detailed for sorting and packing has one particular type of work. In this way men take greater interest and become more or less expert; a larger output and greater efficiency should in consequence result.

51. With this object, separate sections should be organized to deal with the various classes of material. For instance, clothing, blankets and horse rugs might form one section, arms and equipment another, and so on.

52. A non-commissioned officer, or private with a temporary lance-stripe, should be placed in charge of each section, with one or more permanent sorters and packers under him.

53. Sections should be so organized that they can be split into two echelons, as it may be necessary, especially during an advance, to open new Main Salvage Dumps before all material has been evacuated from the old dumps.

Accounts.

54. Salvage Officers will keep a general receipt and expense account of all articles handled by them :—

(i.) Non-commissioned officers in charge of sorting sections will hand in daily checks of articles received.

The receipt side of the account will be compiled from these checks.

(ii.) The expense side of the account will be compiled from receipts for articles issued; and the waybills for all articles despatched for repair or produce.

Returns.

55. To ensure that results obtained balance the labour employed, Divisions will render weekly to Corps Headquarters, on the form given in Appendix III., returns for their area, showing :—

(i.) Articles salved.

(ii.) Cases of apparently preventable waste, so that responsibility may be traced.

56. Corps Troops Area Salvage Officers and Salvage Officers on the Lines of Communication will render similar returns to Corps Headquarters and Headquarters Lines of Communication, respectively.

57. Each Corps will render weekly to the Controller of Salvage, G.H.Q., on A.F. W.3771 (Appendix III.), a return of material received at, and despatched from, Main Salvage Dumps. This will be compiled by summarizing the accounts of the Divisional and Area Salvage Officers.

58. Armies and Headquarters, Lines of Communication, will render similar returns to the Controller of Salvage each week, that rendered by Armies being for the areas not included in the Corps returns under para. 57.

59. These returns will also include a list of the locations of all Main Salvage Dumps in the areas concerned.

60. It should be remembered that, except in the case of battlefield areas, collection of a large quantity of Salvage in an area is a slur on the discipline and interior economy of the units in occupation. The object of Salvage is not a large return, but a clean area.

Duties of Salvage Officers.

Staff Captain (Salvage) at Army Headquarters.

61. The duties of the Staff Captain at Army Headquarters are :—

(i.) Organization and systematization of Salvage operations in the Army Area.

(ii.) Co-ordination of arrangement for road transport.

(iii.) Allotment of any additional labour available.

(iv.) Instructions to Area Commandants and Town Majors.

(v.) Arrangements with Civil Authorities regarding stores left in towns and villages.

(vi.) Returns of material salved in Army Back Area.

62. He should periodically inspect Corps Areas and hold conferences for :—

(i.) Questions of policy to be discussed, so that continuity of action may be secured.

(ii.) Mutual assistance to be arranged so that the greatest value be obtained from labour and transport at disposal of the Salvage Officers in his area.

(iii.) Ideas to be interchanged in order that the system upon which salvage operations are conducted may be improved and standardized.

(iv.) Any matter of importance to be brought forward and fully considered.

Staff Captain (Salvage) at Corps Headquarters.

63. The Staff Captain (Salvage) at Corps Headquarters will organize and control the whole of the salvage operations in the Corps area; he will deal direct with the Corps Troops Area Salvage Officer, but with Divisional Salvage Officers through the Divisional Staffs. To perform his duties efficiently he must :—

(i.) Be continually moving about his area.

(ii.) Be thoroughly acquainted with the traffic circuits and other transport arrangements in his area.

(iii.) Keep in close touch with the Divisional Staffs in his area, and with the representatives of Administrative Services and Departments.

(iv.) Frequently inspect the Salvage Dumps in his area.

(v.) See that salvage does not accumulate at railheads or in dumps. Salved material must be put into circulation with as little delay as possible.

(vi.) Ensure that labour is employed to the best advantage; to this end the following principles should be followed:—

(*A*) A detailed and careful inspection should be made of areas over which salvage operations are to take place, before the salvage personnel is located therein, in order that:—

(*a*) Places where large quantities of salvable material are in sight and easily collected may be worked before others where salvage is less, and so harder to collect.

(*b*) When necessary, priority may be given to the salvage most important at the time.

(*c*) Light railways and transport may be used to the best advantage.

(*d*) "Salvage Receiving Stations" and Main Dumps may be established in the most convenient places.

(*B*) A set task should be given to the salvage personnel weekly.

(*C*) A careful check of work done should be made to determine whether results obtained are commensurate with the labour employed.

(vii.) Keep up to date a large scale map of their areas upon which will be marked:—

(*a*) Gun positions showing whether Field, Heavy or Siege Artillery.

(*b*) Ammunition refilling points.

(*c*) "Salvage Receiving Stations" and Main Salvage Dumps.

(*d*) Dumps of Engineering or other stores.

(*e*) Location of uncollected salvage.

(*f*) Areas clear of salvage.

64. When Special Area Salvage operations on any portion of a Corps or Army Area are to be undertaken, the Staff Captain (Salvage) will forward to the Controller of Salvage:—

(1) A map of that portion of the area, with the above information marked on it.

(2) A report on the estimated quantity of material to be collected and moved at each place and on existing means and difficulties of transportation.

Corps Area and Divisional Officers.

65. The Corps Troops Area Salvage Officer will work directly under, and be responsible to, the Staff Captain (Salvage) at Corps Headquarters. He will report to him all cases of preventable waste or any other necessary matter.

66. The Divisional Salvage Officer will work under instructions from Divisional Headquarters.

67. Corps Troops Area and Divisional Salvage Officers will see that Salvage does not accumulate at "Salvage Receiving Stations," and that Salvage

collected along the sides of light railways and roads is conveyed to Main Dumps without unnecessary delay. Should they be unable to obtain the necessary transport, they will report the matter to Corps or Divisional Headquarters respectively.

68. They will keep a diary in which they will note daily :—

(i.) The work performed by their men.

(ii.) Areas personally inspected.

(iii.) Any matter of interest or point to be brought to notice.

Officers in General.

69. The personal element is the main factor of success: energy must be combined with tact. Salvage Officers must assist Staff Officers of the various formations to stop preventable waste, and at the same time they must help units by making it as easy as possible for them to dispose of legitimate Salvage.

70. They must remember that, until salved material has actually been brought into use, it has only a potential value. Hence, it is of first importance that personnel should be allotted to the various duties of collection, handling and sorting in such proportion as will enable material to be despatched for reissue or repair at practically the same rate as it is collected.

71. Salvage Officers must aim at obtaining the maximum output from the means at their disposal. They should try to originate methods and devices to economize labour. A good system of work in which every man knows his place and duties is essential in every phase of Salvage operations. But it is not enough to rest content with the good: the best alone spells finality.

III.—Special Area Salvage.

1. "Special Area Salvage" is confined to localities specifically named by the Quartermaster General at General Headquarters. The greater part of the work is technical, and can only be satisfactorily directed and supervised by specially qualified officers and men; therefore only broad principles for the general organization of the work are contained in the following paragraphs.

2. Its main objects are :—

(i.) To recover timber and other materials which have been used in the construction of defensive positions, mine-galleries, etc.

(ii.) To dismantle water and telegraph systems.

(iii.) To take down hutments.

Personnel belonging to the various branches of the service concerned will, as far as they are available and required, be attached to the Special Area Salvage organization to supply technical knowledge for the direction and supervision of these duties.

3. In addition to the above, the Special Area Salvage Officer will also :—

(i.) Be responsible for the collection of all derelict material in his area.

(ii.) Assist Area Commandants and Town Majors by provision of labour and transport for removal of salvage collected by them.

4. Under instructions from the Controller of Salvage at General Headquarters he will arrange for the disposal of all material he recovers and collects

5. "Special Area Salvage" operations differ fundamentally from those of "Routine Salvage" in that :—

(i.) They are carried out so far behind the battle line as to be practically free from interruption by the enemy.

(ii.) The labour and transport, whilst at the disposal of the Special Area Salvage Officer, is specifically allotted to this work, and has no other duties.

(iii.) Except in case of a retirement, they are unaffected by movements of troops and so stop in an area until the work is done.

6. For these reasons, they can be organized on consecutive lines to secure absolutely methodical clearance of the ground.

7. In the first place, a map survey, map square by map square, should be made of the whole of the Special Salvage Area, and the estimated tonnage of salvable material in each square recorded on the map. The area should then be divided into sub-areas; the number of sub-areas depending on road and railway facilities and the amount of material to be handled.

8. Skilled supervision, transport and labour, will be allotted to sub-areas by the Special Area Salvage Officer in proportion to :—

(i.) The amount and nature of the material to be salved.

(ii.) The means for its evacuation and disposal.

9. A Special Sub-Area Salvage Officer will be appointed to organize the work in each sub-area. A copy of the map survey for his sub-area should be given to him.

10. He will allot work to the ~~various~~ Labour Units and will apportion the skilled supervision and transport among them. It is most important that the allotment of labour, skilled supervision, and transport to each task be properly co-ordinated, in order that the fullest value may be obtained from each and all of them.

11. Material collected for conveyance to the dumps should be stacked by categories, such as Engineering, Ordnance, Supply Stores, etc. The various types of articles should also be kept distinct from each other and a separate heap made for each type.

12. Similarly, material should be loaded for despatch to the dumps by categories, and articles of the same type kept together as far as possible.

13. The Special Area Salvage Officer will establish such dumps as are necessary for reception, sorting and disposal of salved material.

14. An officer will be placed in charge of each dump. He will be responsible for its organization and the care of all material received by him.

15. Careful organization in the beginning means economy of labour and time in the end. Engineering, Ordnance and Supply Stores, etc., should invariably be kept separate and a particular portion of the dump allotted to each.

16. The "lay-out" of a dump should be such as entails the minimum amount of labour to handle the various stores in and out of the dump.

IV.—The Disposal of Salved Stores at Bases.

1. Salved stores which are not required for local reissue are consigned to the appropriate Depots at the various Bases. There, however, the term "Salvage" is somewhat differently understood. In the forward area all derelict

material becomes Salvage, as distinct from Returned Stores, even although it be in quite serviceable condition. At the Bases this distinction is of very secondary importance, and serviceable and repairable stores are added to stock for reissue whether they were evacuated as salved material or as stores returned by units through the normal channels of supply. Conversely, unserviceable material is disposed of under the heading "Salvage" without regard to the channel through which it was received.

2. This difference in classification and nomenclature has been rendered inevitable by the fundamental fact that those concerned with the collection of material must chiefly consider the question of its origin, while those concerned with the disposal of material must chiefly consider its nature and condition. To meet this position the following definitions of "Salvage," in its two aspects, have been definitely laid down.

3. "Outside the Depot of a Service or Department 'Salvage' comprises all materials and stores, of whatsoever kind and in whatever condition, that pass through a Salvage Dump, or are collected by Salvage personnel or under the orders of a Salvage Officer (Executive or Staff)."

4. "Inside the Depots of Services or Departments, 'Salvage' comprises—

(i.) All material of whatever nature, when reduced to produce or scrap.

(ii.) All empties which are not required for refilling in this country by the Department which holds them.

(iii.) All by-products, after recovery by the Department concerned.

(iv.) Serviceable stores which are for local disposal and for which the Department concerned has no outlet."

5. As a result of the second of these definitions, it has been decided that Departments and Services will include all such produce, scrap, empties and by-products in their return A.F. W.3772 (Appendix IV.), to be rendered weekly to the Controller of Salvage, shewing how any portions have been disposed of and what remain for disposal by the Controller of Salvage. Consequent on this, a Service or Department will not make any sales of any of the above material without instructions from the Controller of Salvage.

6. Each Department has the first claim on its own Salvage material, either for use in its workshops in France or for despatch to the corresponding department at Home. All material thus disposed of, however, has to be accounted for on the weekly Salvage returns.

7. When no departmental outlet exists, it rests with the Controller of Salvage to ascertain how the material may most economically be disposed of, and to issue the necessary instructions. Preference is given to the needs of other Departments in France, and it is frequently found that one Department can use in its workshops scrap material for which the holding Department can find no use.

8. Failing any such method of disposal, inquiries are made as to whether the material is required for any purpose in the United Kingdom, and, if so, whether it would be economical to ship it. Should this outlet also be closed, the material is sold in France at the best price obtainable.

9. The following table shews in brief how some of the principal items of salved stores are dealt with or disposed of. The table includes the treatment of repairable stores although these cease to be considered as Salvage, as explained above, on arrival at the Base. All possible repairs are made in France

by the Departments concerned, it may be added, with a view to economizing handling, transport, and freight, and to bringing the damaged articles into use again with the least delay. More elaborate repairs, however, can be carried out at Home. Special reference is made to the repair of ammunition components in Section V. below.

Nature of Material.	*How dealt with.*
R.A.F. STORES :	
Aeroplane stores R.A.F. mechanical transport stores Instruments	Repaired in R.A.F. Workshops. Unserviceable material utilized in repair work or disposed of as scrap.
Balloon fabric.	Used for making small nurse balloons, etc.
By-products of hydrogen manufacture.	*See* Section VI., para. 6.
ENGINEERING STORES :	
e.g., timber, corrugated iron, tools, sandbags, piping, bridging material.	Repaired in R.E. workshops. Unserviceable material utilized in repair work or disposed of as scrap. The bulk of salved stores of this nature, however, are fit for immediate local reissue.
Cement casks.	*See* G.R.O. 4921.
Camouflage material.	*See* G.R.O. 4264.
TRANSPORTATION STORES :	
e.g., railway material.	Repaired in the workshops of the Transportation Services. Unserviceable material utilized in repair work or disposed of as scrap.
SIGNALLING STORES :	
e.g., wire, cable, cable drums, poles, instruments.	Dealt with by the Signal Service.
ELECTRICAL STORES :	Dealt with by Electrical and Mechanical Companies, R.E. (*see* G.R.O.s 2245 and 5304). Exhausted accumulators and batteries are returned to U.K. for disposal (*see* G.R.O. 4689).
TANK STORES :	Repaired in Tank Corps Workshops. Unserviceable material utilized in repair work or disposed of as scrap. The Corps possesses a special organization for Salvage work in the field.
SUPPLIES :	
Damaged food-stuffs, offal, skins, bakery sweepings, etc.	Used as food for animals or sold to the French trade. Some bakery sweepings are used for making adhesive paste for Army purposes, and for horse and pig food.
Fat and bones.	Prepared and shipped to U.K. *See* Section VI., para. 3.

Nature of Material.	*How dealt with.*
SUPPLIES—continued :—	
Empties (*e.g.*, crates, cases, sacks, wrappers, barrels, drums, rum jars).	The majority are used for refilling, either at Base Supply Depots or in U.K. Certain types of crates can be broken down into "shooks" for ready transportation. Tins, other than serviceable or repairable petrol tins, are not so used. (*See* below.) Lead linings of tea boxes are rendered down. (*See* G.R.O. 5162.)
Jam cartons.	Returned to U.K. for pulping. (*See* G.R.O.s 4948 and 4999.)
MECHANICAL TRANSPORT STORES :	Repaired in A.S.C. Workshops. Unserviceable material utilized in repair work or disposed of as scrap.
MEDICAL STORES :	
Instruments and equipment.	Dealt with in R.A.M.C. Workshops at Base Depots of Medical Stores.
Empties (*e.g.*, bottles, boxes, wrappers).	Returned to manufacturers for refilling.
Used surgical dressings.	If unfit for reuse, but capable of sterilization, these are disposed of as cotton waste.
VETERINARY STORES :	
Instruments, equipment & empties.	Dealt with by A.V.D.
Animals fit only for civil work.	Sold to French civilian buyers.
Animals unfit for work.	Slaughtered for food for P. of W. Companies or sold to the French for slaughtering.
Animals unfit for food.	Used for recovery of by-products.
By-products, (*e.g.*, hides, hair, hooves, fat, bones).	*See* Section VI., para. 4.
AMMUNITION :	
Defective ammunition.	Repaired in A.O.D. Depots or in U.K.
Unserviceable or obsolete ammunition.	Broken down for recovery of constituents (*see* Section VI., para. 5).
Empties and components.	Shipped to U.K. for reuse in munition factories. For instructions as to sorting and packing *see* G.R.O. 4513. For details of disposal *see* Section V. below.
S.A.A.	Sufficient cleaned and retained for training purposes; remainder boxed and sent Home. German S.A.A. is also sent to U.K. *N.B.*—Attention is drawn to the importance of ensuring that no live ammunition or explosives are included in consignments of ammunition empties, scrap metal, or other salvage material.

Nature of Material.	*How dealt with.*
RDNANCE STORES:	
Guns.	Repaired in Ordnance Workshops. If beyond repair sent to the U.K.; if irreparable, disposed of as steel scrap.
Machine guns, Lewis guns, rifles, pistols, etc.	Repaired in Ordnance Workshops. If beyond local repair, sent to the U.K. The smallest components are recovered and nothing is scrapped, except steel portions of the Lewis machine gun magazine, which are disposed of as scrap steel. Especial care should be taken of machine gun locks and lock covers.
Bayonets.	Repaired in Ordnance Workshops. If irreparable, sent to the U.K.
Pull through weights.	Fitted with new cords.
Oil bottles.	Cleaned.
Limbers, gun carriages, etc.	Repaired in Ordnance Workshops. If beyond local repair, sent to the U.K. If irreparable, disposed of as scrap metal after removal of any utilizable part.
Vehicles (horse transport).	Repaired in Ordnance Workshops. Utilizable parts of irreparable vehicles removed and kept as spares.
Wheels.	Repaired in Ordnance Workshops. If beyond local repair, sent to the U.K. If irreparable, scrapped. Iron tyres and hubs sent to the U.K. Wood utilized for making tent pegs.
Fittings from bars supporting draught poles, etc.	Returned to the U.K.
Horseshoes.	Classified: if "new," packed for re-issue at the Front; if "fit for further wear," issued for use on L. of C.; if unfit for further use, disposed of as scrap metal.
Horseshoe nails.	Cleaned in rumblers and sized.
Chains, buckles, bits, etc.	Cleaned in rumblers.
Spurs.	New rowels inserted.
Leather equipment, harness, saddlery, etc.	Broken down into component parts, washed with soft soap in lukewarm water, dried in a drying cupboard at 100 deg. F., treated with fish oil, and repaired. If irreparable, sent to the U.K. as old leather after brass or metal fittings have been removed.

Nature of Material.	*How dealt with.*
ORDNANCE STORES—continued :—	
Boots.	Classified, repaired and passed through fish-oil bath. The uppers of irreparable boots are, as far as possible, made into shoe laces or heel lifts, and used for filling. Remainder sold to the French trade.
Web equipment, cotton bandoliers, etc.	Broken into component parts, dry cleaned on motor driven brushes, darned and repaired. If irreparable, sent to the U.K. as cotton rags, after brass or metal fittings have been removed.
Water bottles.	Old felt removed, bottles cleaned, recovered with new felt, and recorked. Old felt sent to the U.K. Water-bottles not fit for reissue as such are used for packing small quantities of oil or paint for the Front.
Mess tins, camp kettles, field kitchen boilers.	Cleaned in caustic soda, reblocked, resoldered if necessary, and retinned. If irreparable, disposed of as scrap metal.
Knives, forks and spoons.	Cleaned and reissued.
Box respirators.	Broken down and valuable component parts, *e.g.*, the mask pipes, sent to U.K.
Steel helmets.	Cleaned and relined. If irreparable, indiarubber pads in linings removed and utilized for lining serviceable helmets; chin strap sold as old leather, and helmet disposed of as steel scrap.
Entrenching tools.	Heads cleaned and sharpened. If irreparable, disposed of as scrap.
Clothing.	Cleaned and repaired locally. If beyond repair, sent to the U.K. as rags.
Sacking.	Sent to the U.K.
Optical instruments, watches, etc.	Repaired in Ordnance Workshops. If beyond local repair, sent to the U.K.
Bicycles.	Repaired in Ordnance Workshops. If beyond local repair, sent to the U.K. If irreparable, disposed of as scrap, after any portion that can be utilized has been removed.
Rubber (gum boots, tyres, etc.).	Sent to Paris for classification and repair. If irreparable, sent to the U.K.

Nature of Material.	*How dealt with.*
SCRAP MATERIAL AND MISCELLANEOUS:	
Scrap metal.	Used in workshops as far as possible. When one department cannot utilize its scrap another frequently has a use for it, and a transfer is effected through the medium of the Salvage Control. The remaining scrap, except certain valuable categories which are shipped to U.K., is sold to the French Government under a standing agreement. Technical scrap, such as mechanical transport parts or railway material, is not treated as scrap unless rejected as unserviceable by the Service concerned. Instructions for sorting and evacuation are given in G.R.O.s 4704 and 5002, and in Q.M.G. Circular 4000/6 (Q.B.1) of 28-8-18. For special instructions regarding the recovery of tin-plate from old tins *see* G.R.O. 5162 and the publication therein referred to. For the recovery of solder, *see* Section VI., paras. 1 and 2.
Scrap wood.	Used in workshops. If unserviceable, issued as fuel.
Waste paper.	Sorted, baled and shipped to U.K. for repulping.
Rags.	Shipped to U.K. for sale to the trade. Woollen rags are especially valuable.
Unserviceable sacking ("gunny").	Shipped to U.K. for paper manufacture.
Bottles.	Shipped to U.K. packed in A.S.C. "Empties" (*see* G.R.O. 4689).
Broken glass.	Sold to French trade.
Used photographic negatives.	Shipped to U.K. for use as eye-pieces of box respirators.
Scrap celluloid.	Shipped to U.K.
Scrap rubber.	Shipped to U.K.
Scrap leather.	Shipped to U.K. or sold to the French trade.
By-products.	*See* Section VI. below.
STORES OF ALLIED ARMIES:	Returned to original owners in terms of a reciprocal agreement.
CAPTURED STORES:	Utilized for any purpose for which they are suitable, or disposed of as scrap.

V.—Disposal of Ammunition Empties and Components Returned to the United Kingdom.

1. Various depots and factories have been established in the United Kingdom for dealing with material returned from France.

2. Every effort is made to bring it into circulation with as little delay as possible.

3. Articles beyond repair, or useless in their present form, are brought to produce.

4. Government factories for the reformation of Q.F. cartridge cases and repair of Q.F. ammunition boxes are now in operation. With the exception of a few men for upkeep of machinery, etc., the labour is entirely female, and mechanical labour-saving devices are employed to the fullest extent.

5. The factories are fed from the stacking grounds at the wharf by a combination of electric conveyors and gravity rollers. In the shops, also, the cartridge cases are carried from one machine to another, and through the various processes of washing and annealing, by electric conveyors.

6. In fact, it may be said that the reformation of cartridge cases is organized on the same principles as the construction of a Ford car; they come into one end of the shop as so much seemingly useless scrap, but arrive at the other end ready for service.

7. The following is the process by which 18-pounder and other fired brass cartridge cases are reformed:—

(i.) The primer is extracted in a special machine at the rate of 520 per hour.

(ii.) The worst dents are removed on an anvil with a wooden mallet.

(iii.) Preliminary washing both in a tank and on a special washing machine fitted with rotating brushes.

(iv.) Passed on an endless chain through an annealing furnace and annealed 3-in. downwards from the mouth.

(v.) Passed through a rolling machine to take out all dents.

(vi.) Put back to size in a power press, which is capable of sizing 540 cases in an hour.

(vii.) Any distortion due to firing, etc., is corrected on a special lathe.

(viii.) Final washing, similar to the first process, *i.e.*, they are passed through tanks on endless chains.

8. Reformed cartridge cases are taken to the Inspection Benches, and, if passed, are stacked at the end of the shop ready to be packed into the repaired ammunition boxes in which they are sent to the filling factories.

9. Each line of machinery is capable of reforming about 500 cases an hour.

10. The repair of boxes is conducted on similar lines, as follows:—

(i.) All defects are made good.

(ii.) New wires are fitted.

(iii.) The old stencilling is painted out.

11. The boxes are then examined by the Inspection Department. If passed, they are sent where the reformed cartridge cases are stacked, to act as transit cases to the filling factories. There they are reïssued after being filled with complete rounds.

12. The following table shews how the various components are dealt with:—

Component.	How dealt with.
Empty shrapnel shell bodies	Brought to produce.
Q.F. gun brass cartridge cases	Reformed.
,, ,, ,, ,, clips	Reformed.
Cartridge cylinders	Reformed.
Transit plugs	Rectified.
Primers*	Rectified.
Ammunition boxes	Repaired.
Metal-lined powder cases	Repaired.
Projectile slings	Repaired.
Grenade boxes, etc.	Repaired.
Fuze caps...	Brought to produce.
Fired S.A.A. cartridges	Brought to produce.
Live S.A.A.	Cleaned and, if necessary, recapped.
Cordite rings	Regraded.
Fuze tins	Inspected; if unfit for further use, sold.

* A primer can only be rectified once, after which it is brought to produce.

13. Below are a few examples of the money saved by repair of salved articles of this nature:—

Item	Cost of repair	Value new	Net gain
18-pdr. C.C.	1·755d.	8s.	7s. 10·245d.
4·5 C.C.	2d.	8s.	7s. 10d.
18-pdr. boxes	2s.	5s.	3s.
4·5 boxes	9d.	4s.	3s. 3d.
Clips, 18-pdr.	2s. 1d. per 100.	18s. 8d. per 100.	16s. 7d per 100.
Friction tubes	9½d. per 100.	£5 10s. per 100.	£5 9s. 2½d. per 100.

VI.—The Recovery of By-Products.

1. The most widespread by-product process being carried on in France is the recovery of solder from empty tins. The material for this is naturally available everywhere, the necessary kilns are easily constructed, and the amount of labour and fuel required is comparatively small. The results are already highly satisfactory, and the total amount recovered by units during the five weeks ending 31st August, 1918, was 15 tons, valued at £2,700.

2. As a result of experiments the general adoption of two alternative types of solder kiln is recommended. The first is the "Beehive" kiln, a solid brick structure suitable for large standing camps and also useful as a refuse destructor. The other is a corrugated iron device of very simple construction, and particularly adapted to the needs of small and mobile units. Illustrated directions for the construction and use of these kilns have been separately published. Information on such points is also obtainable from the Controller

of Salvage, at whose Headquarters examples of solder kilns and other devices may be seen.

3. The extraction of fat from kitchen waste, and the preparation of bones for shipment, are carried out under the control of the I.Q.M.G.S. (M. and E.). Ellis Field Fat Extracting Plants for this purpose are situated at various places on the L. of C. Dripping rendered down by units in the forward areas is also returned to these installations.

The bulk of the material is shipped Home for munition purposes, and a total of 1,070 tons was disposed of during the five weeks ending 31st August, 1918. The money realized by the sales is paid out to the units which return the material, and does not, therefore, represent a financial gain to the State. The recovery is nevertheless highly important as a source of valuable material.

4. The Veterinary Services possess a system for the recovery of all possible by-products and have a number of "Economizer Plants" on the L. of C. The material recovered includes hides, hair, hooves, fat, bones, dessicated meat, and manure. Units in the field and out of reach of these plants return what they can themselves recover, principally hides. The total value realized by the recovery of these by-products, and by the sale of cast animals, was over £31,000 for the five weeks ending 31st August, 1918.

5. Certain by-products are recovered by the A.O.D. from defective and obsolete grenades and other ammunition. These include potassium nitrate, pitch, and various metals. Instructions for the recovery of shellac from unserviceable ground flares are contained in G.R.O. 5142.

6. Among other by-products that may be mentioned are those of the manufacture of hydrogen for R.A.F. Kite-Balloons. These consist chiefly of sodium silicate (waterglass) and a vaseline grease. Both substances are recovered by the Salvage organization, the former being disposed of to the Engineer Services as a fire-proofing agent and as a basis for the manufacture of paints, and the latter being purified by the A.S.C. for use as an M.T. lubricant.

SALVAGE ORGANIZATION FOR THE FORCE.

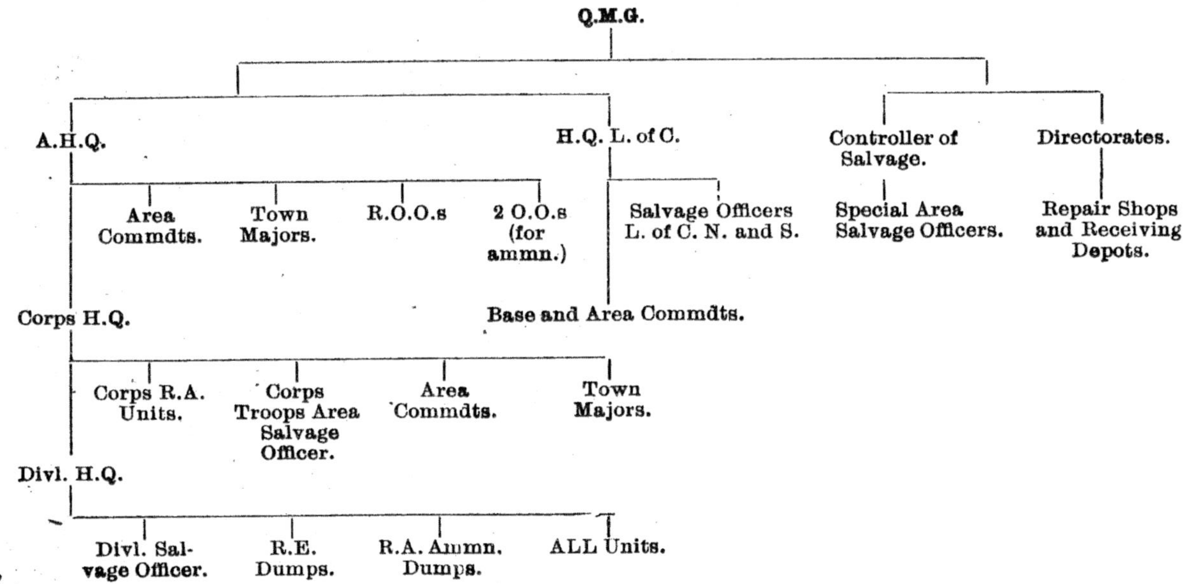

APPENDIX II.

ORGANIZATION OF SALVAGE UNITS FOR A CORPS CONSISTING OF THREE DIVISIONS.

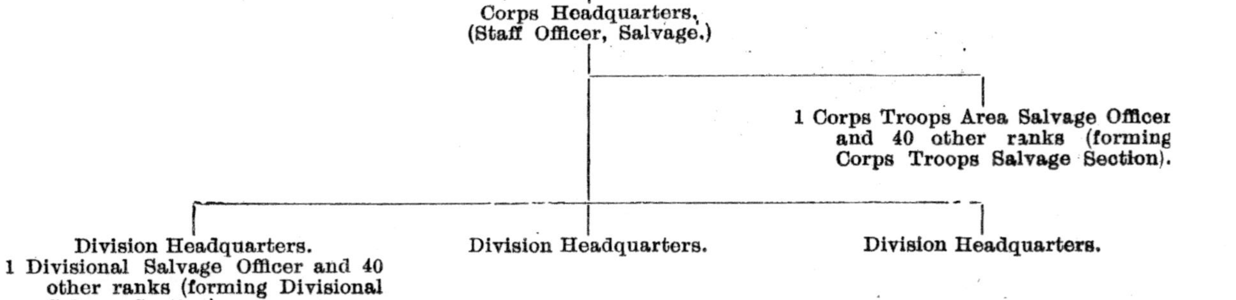

APPENDIX III.

Army Form W. 3771.

RETURN OF SALVAGE.

Received and disposed of at Salvage Dumps during week ending Saturday..............................

FORMATION..............................

Article.	Unit of Measure.	Stock on hand previous week.	Receipts during week.	Amount disposed of		Stock on hand at date.	REMARKS.
				Re-issued locally.	Evacuated to Base.		
(1)	(2)	(3)	(4)	(5)	(6)	(7)	(8)
							(In cases of apparently preventable waste, localities where articles have been salved should appear in this column.

NOTE.—Articles should be described as accurately as possible, and should be enumerated in the order shown in the pamphlet "Headings under which salved material should be recorded and 'unit of measure' to be adopted in all returns." This pamphlet is obtainable from the Controller of Salvage. It is not complete and can only be taken as a guide.

DEPOTS. APPENDIX IV. Army Form W.3772.

STATEMENT OF RECEIPTS AND DISPOSALS OF SALVAGE MATERIAL.

To be completed up to midnight on Saturday and forwarded to Controller of Salvage, G.H.Q., by Tuesday each week.

Weights shown should be in D.W. Tonnage. **Depot.................................** **Week Ending ....191...**

Description of Article.	Commencing Stock.	Receipts.	Disposals.									Closing Stock.
			To U.K.	Port in U.K.	Consignee.	Name of Ship or Number of Barge or Train Ferry Truck.	Date Sailed.	Used in Work-shops.	To Store or Re-issued.	Sold Locally	Total.	
1	2	3	4	5	6	7	8	9	10	11	12	13

ND - #0529 - 270225 - C0 - 195/127/3 - PB - 9781908487650 - Matt Lamination